The Selected Poems of
Li Po

OTHER TRANSLATIONS BY

DAVID HINTON

The Selected Poems of
Li Po

TRANSLATED BY

DAVID HINTON

A NEW DIRECTIONS BOOK

ACKNOWLEDGMENTS
The translation of this book was supported by grants from the National
Endowment for the Humanities and the Witter Bynner Foundation.

Some of these poems first appeared in *The American Poetry Review.*

Manufactured in the United States of America

First published as New Directions Paperbook 823 in 1996

Book design and map by Sylvia Frezzolini Severance

Library of Congress Cataloging-in-Publication Data
Li Po, d701-762
    [Poems. English. Selections]
    The selected poems of Li Po / translated by David Hinton.
        p. cm.
    "A New directions book."
    Includes bibliographical references.
        ISBN-13: 978-0-8112-1323-3   ISBN-10:0-8112-1323-4
    1. Li, Po, d701-762—Translations into English. I. Hinton,
    David, 1954 - .   II. Title.
    PL2671.A25 1996
      895.1' 13—dc20   96-5139
                                                       CIP

New Directions Books are published for James Laughlin
By New Directions Publishing Corporation,
80 Eighth Avenue, New York, NY 10011

SEVENTEENTH PRINTING

CONTENTS

The Selected Poems of
Li Po

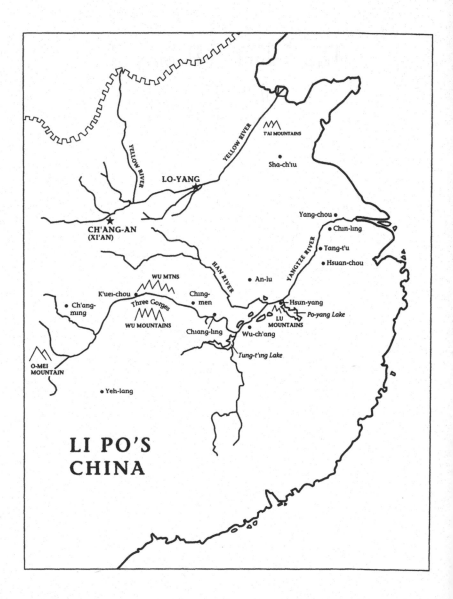

YELLOW RIVER

YELLOW RIVER

T'AI MOUNTAINS

Sha-ch'iu

LO-YANG

Yang-chou

CH'ANG-AN
(XI'AN)

Chin-ling

Tang-t'u

Hsuan-chou

HAN RIVER

An-lu

YANGTZE RIVER

WU MTNS

K'uei-chou

Ching-
men

Ch'ang-
ming

Three Gorges

Hsun-yang

Po-yang Lake

WU MOUNTAINS

LU
MOUNTAINS

Chiang-ling

Wu-ch'ang

O-MEI
MOUNTAIN

Tung-t'ing Lake

Yeh-lang

LI PO'S
CHINA

INTRODUCTION

I. THE WORK

There is a set-phrase in Chinese referring to the phenomenon of Li Po: "Winds of the immortals, bones of the Tao." He is called the "Banished Immortal," an exiled spirit moving through this world with an unearthly ease and freedom from attachment. But at the same time, he belongs to earth in the most profound way, for he is also free of attachments to self, and that allows the self to blend easily into a weave of identification with the earth and its process of change: the earth perpetually moving beyond itself as the ten thousand things unfold spontaneously, each according to its own nature.

In Chinese, this unfolding is *tzu-jan:* literally "self-so" or "being such of itself," hence "natural" or "spontaneous." Li Po's work is suffused with the wonder of being part of this process, but at the same time, he *enacts* it, makes it visible in the self-dramatized spontaneity of his life. To live as part of the earth's process of change is to live one's most authentic self: rather than acting with self-conscious intention, one acts with selfless spontaneity. This spontaneity is *wu-wei* (literally: "doing nothing"), and it is an important part of Taoist and Ch'an (Zen) practice, the way to experience one's life as an organic part of *tzu-jan*. Educated Chinese had always been imbued with Taoist philosophy, and Ch'an had become very influential among the intellectuals of Li Po's time, many of whom associated with Ch'an monks and spent time in Ch'an monasteries. *Wu-wei* was therefore a widely-held ideal, appearing most famously in "wild-grass" calligraphy (begun by Chang Hsü and Huai Su, friends of Li Po who would get drunk and, in a sudden flurry, create a flowing landscape of virtually indecipherable characters), in the antics of Ch'an masters, and in Li Po himself.

But for Li Po, it seems not so much a spiritual practice as the inborn form of his life, much of which was spent wandering. As this was primarily wandering on whim rather than traveling of necessity, it gives his life the very shape of spontaneity: sailing downriver hundreds of miles in a day or settling in one place for a year. Li Po's spontaneity also takes the form of wild drinking and a gleeful disdain for decorum and authority, as in the story where he fails to pay the proper respects when being introduced to a governor and, upon being reprimanded, quips: "Wine makes its own manners." Li Po's poetry was itself often intended to shock his readers, and he was considered outlandish by the decorous literary society of his time. But it was in another aspect of his writing that Li Po embodies the principle of *wu-wei* in a more fundamental way: the headlong movement of the poem and its gestures. This movement is a natural result of the spontaneous composition process which is a major part of the Li Po legend. The story recurs in many forms, perhaps most famously in Tu Fu's "Song of the Eight Immortals in Wine":

> For Li Po, it's a hundred poems per gallon of wine,
> then sleep in the winehouses of Ch'ang-an markets.

The most essential quality of Li Po's work is the way in which *wu-wei* spontaneity gives shape to his experience of the natural world. He is primarily engaged by the natural world in its wild, rather than domestic forms. Not only does the wild evoke wonder, it is also where the spontaneous energy of *tzu-jan* is clearly visible, energy with which Li Po identified. And the spontaneous movement of a Li Po poem literally enacts this identification, this belonging to earth in the fundamental sense of belonging to its processes.

Li Po wrote during the High T'ang period (A.D. 712-760) when Chinese poetry blossomed into its first full splendor, and he is one of the High T'ang's three preeminent poets, Wang Wei and Tu Fu being the other two. A major catalyst in the High T'ang revolution was admiration for a poet who had been neglected since his death three hundred years earlier: T'ao Ch'ien (365-427), the poet of "fields and gardens." Wang Wei, Li Po, and Tu Fu are all direct heirs to T'ao Ch'ien's resolute individuality and authentic human voice. But Li Po is no less heir to Hsieh Ling-yün (385-433), the poet of wild "mountains and rivers." *Mountains* were not merely natural, but sacred objects. Quite literally sites where the powers of heaven met those of earth, they were inhabited and energized by those powers. *Rivers* formed part of a single cosmic watershed. Beginning in western mountains where the Star River (our Milky Way) descends to earth, they flow east toward the sea, and there ascend to become again the earth-cradling Star River. And together "mountains and rivers" literally means "landscape," wild landscape as a truly numinous phenomenon.

The moon, though, absorbed the Banished Immortal utterly. Appearing in over a third of his poems, it is a beacon from his homeland. It's difficult for us now to imagine what the moon was for T'ang intellectuals, but it was not in any sense the celestial body that we know. In a universe animated by the interaction of *yin* (female) and *yang* (male) energies, the moon was literally *yin* visible. Indeed, it was the very germ or source of *yin*, and the sun was its *yang* counterpart. Like all other natural phenomena, a person's spirit was thought to be made up of these two aspects. It took the form of two distinct spirits: the *yin* spirit, which was called *p'o* and remained earthbound at death, and the *yang* spirit, which was called *hun* and drifted away into the heavens at death. The moon, too, was known as *p'o* or *yin-p'o*. Hence, the moon was the heavenly incarnation of, was indeed the embryonic essence of that mysterious energy we call the spirit (*yin* spirit, with the sun being the source of *yang* spirit). This is the conceptual context within which Li Po's poems operate, the culture's account of the moon's mystery. But rather than account for it, the poems themselves evoke it directly, evoke it and yet leave it as it is, even now: an enduring mystery.

With the moon, inevitably, comes wine. Drinking

plays an important part in the lives of most Chinese poets, acting as a form of enlightenment comparable to Ch'an practice. But only T'ao Ch'ien is as closely identified with the "sage in the cup" as Li Po. Usually in Chinese poetry, the practice of wine involves drinking just enough so the ego fades and perception is clarified. T'ao Ch'ien called this state "idleness" (*hsien*): *wu-wei* as stillness. But although Li Po certainly cultivates such stillness, he usually ends up thoroughly drunk, a state in which he is released fully into his most authentic and enlightened self: *wu-wei* as spontaneity.

During China's T'ang Dynasty, a man named Li Po is born in the year 701, at the beginning of the great cultural flowering known as the High T'ang. He wanders. The moon beckons from his homeland, dances with his shadow. The river flows on the borders of heaven. He meets Tu Fu in a country wineshop, and they share a few days. Armies burn fields and cities. The T'ang smolders, a fitful ruin. In 762, Li Po's wandering ends south of the Yangtze River, at someone else's house, when he falls into a river and drowns trying to embrace the moon. The phenomenon of Li Po moves perpetually beyond the everyday facts which make up a life. He belongs at once to the realm of immortals and to the earth's process of change, its spontaneous movement beyond itself. But his most enduring work remains grounded in the everyday experience we all share. He wrote 1200 years ago, half a world away, but in his poems we see our world transformed by winds of the immortals, bones of the Tao.

II. THE LIFE

As with most immortals, the facts of Li Po's existence are nebulous. He was himself the ultimate source for most of the biographical information we have, and with his perpetual self-dramatization, he was a decidedly unreliable source. Fortunately, few of the poems depend on biographical context for their meaning. Although many can be reliably dated, scholars have doubted the authenticity of up to nine-tenths of the poems, making the age-old attempts to guess at their dates especially futile. In spite of the uncertainty, it has seemed best to leave aside the question of authenticity and to arrange the poems in some chronological order, however imaginary that order may be. This is the only way to re-embody the legend that Li Po is, and even if that legend has little to do with historical fact, it is the Li Po that has been revered for 1200 years.

Early Years (A.D.701-742)

Li Po's life begins, suitably enough, nebulous and beyond. He was born outside the boundaries of China, in Central Asia, and his full given name was T'ai-po, meaning "Venus." His great-grandfather had apparently been exiled to Central Asia, and as they found themselves on the trading routes between China and the West, the family may have turned to trading for a livelihood. When Li Po was still young, the family moved to Ch'ang-ming in western China, where they probably continued their trading business. Wanting to create an exotic aura for himself, Li Po promoted his Central Asian background, which may indeed have been a complete fabrication invented by a man of the lower merchant class to give himself an aristocratic pedigree. He claimed the same imaginary genealogy as the imperial family (which also had Central Asian connections), a genealogy reaching back to no less a figure than the mythical Taoist philosopher Lao-tzu (whose family name was Li). Still, evidence such as descriptions of his strange and striking appearance suggest Li Po had much Central Asian blood in him. Indeed, he may not have been Chinese at all.

In any case, Li Po was accepted as part of the far-flung and illustrious Li family, a "cousin" of imperial princes. Most of his relatives were officials in government, some of a fairly high rank. But even though he showed considerable literary talent at a young age, he never studied for the imperial examinations, though that was the normal route to a career in government. If indeed he was a Li, such a career would have been the expected thing for him, the way to secure a place for himself in the world. Instead, he spent some time as a "knight-errant," which involved avenging injustices suffered by the helpless, and it is said that in this role he killed several people with his sword. He also spent several years as a Taoist recluse in the mountains near his home. These two occupations are emblematic of Li Po's temperament: a deep and quiet spirituality on the one hand, and on the other, a swaggering brashness.

Around A.D. 724, Li Po sailed out of Szechwan, his

remote home province in the west, and down the Yangtze River to travel in eastern China. Some years later, he was married and living in An-lu. This began a decade of apparently settled life about which little is known. By the late 730s, his wife and perhaps a son had died, and Li Po had begun in earnest the wandering which dominates his life. This wandering seems to have been carefree, probably supported by the lucrative family business and the relatives with whom he often stayed.

Ch'ang-an and Middle Years (A.D.742-755)

To be a poet in China meant little without a position in the government, for that was the basic source of status and self-esteem. So although Li Po was by now a famous poet, he surely aspired to an official position, and he could have hoped for an appointment outside the usual examination system, on the basis of his extraordinary literary abilities and/or his considerable Taoist expertise. And in 742, through his friendship with a well-known Taoist writer, he received an imperial summons which took him to the capital, Ch'ang-an.

Ch'ang-an, with a population of two million, was perhaps the most cultivated and cosmopolitan city in human history, and T'ang civilization was at its peak. Under Emperor Hsüan-tsung's enthusiastic patronage, arts and letters flourished. Indeed, his reign is often considered the pinnacle of Chinese cultural achievement. The government's frugality and devotion were legendary; corruption was rare and taxation light. Able generals secured the borders against ever-threatening "barbarians," and within China there was peace and prosperity.

Instead of receiving a position in the central government as he must have hoped, Li Po was appointed to the Han-lin Academy, becoming a court poet in attendance on the emperor. His preternatural talents and bold disdain for decorum and authority were a hit, and there are numerous tales of his eccentric behavior in the capital. As at any other time in his life, he was often to be found in winehouses, carousing with courtesans. In a typical story of Li Po's exploits, the poet is summoned to capture the glory of an imperial outing and arrives dead drunk. Attendants throw cold water in his face to rouse him, and he thereupon tosses off a celebrated series of poems. The full account of Li Po in Tu Fu's "Song of the Eight Immortals in Wine" contains another version of this story:

> For Li Po, it's a hundred poems per gallon of wine,
> then sleep in the winehouses of Ch'ang-an markets.
>
> Summoned by the Son of Heaven, he can't board the ship,
> calls himself *your loyal subject immortal in wine*.

Indeed, it was at this time that he received the appellation "Banished Immortal": an immortal who had misbehaved and been sent to earth for punishment. But Li Po's irresponsible antics eventually resulted in his dismissal. Although just what happened is unclear, Li Po was sent from the capital in 744.

He resumed his wandering, soon meeting Tu Fu in a

country wineshop near Lo-yang and traveling with him briefly. Li Po had by now remarried, and the family, which included a daughter and son, was settled at Sha-ch'iu in eastern China. The following year, Tu Fu lived briefly in the same region, and Li Po visited him. Tu Fu is an important part of the Li Po legend. The two of them are traditionally considered the greatest poets in Chinese history, even if such claims are an exaggeration. But this pairing is based on more than their shared pre-eminence. They were friends, and their work is often said to represent the two poles of Chinese sensibility: Li Po being the Taoist (intuitive, amoral, detached), and Tu Fu the Confucian (cerebral, moral, socially-engaged). Informative though it may be, this contrast is a simplifi-cation. To be a complete human being, a Chinese intel-lectual must be both Taoist and Confucian, and this was true of both Li Po and Tu Fu. In any case, the elder Li Po was already quite famous when the two poets met, and the as yet unknown Tu Fu admired him inordinate-ly. But this was to be the last time the two poets would meet. It seems Tu Fu quickly passed from Li Po's mind. Only two of Li Po's surviving poems are addressed to Tu Fu, both occasional poems dating from this period (and typically, one is probably not authentic). But Tu Fu often thought of Li Po, and over the years wrote more than a dozen poems concerning him.

Li Po seems to have spent rather little time with his family over the next decade. Instead, he continued to wander eastern China in fine fashion, accompanied by servants and courtesans. Meanwhile, China suffered several major military setbacks, and criticism of the government's expansionist policies grew. Between 750 and 754, there was an unprecedented series of natural disasters which wreaked havoc upon the common people. Although the government tried to provide disaster relief, it was far from adequate, and popular resentment grew. To make matters worse, the emperor's obsessions turned from art and government to magic elixirs of immortality and his infamous consort, Yang Kuei-fei. He left the affairs of state to a scheming and dangerous prime minister, Li Lin-fu. One of Li Lin-fu's many disastrous actions was to replace loyal military governors whom he could not be certain of controlling with illiterate barbarian generals. Soon, the emperor controlled only the palace army directly, while foreign generals with no real loyalty to the T'ang government controlled vast autonomous armies and territories, setting what should have been an all too obvious stage for the catastrophe soon to follow.

War, Exile, and Later Years (A.D.755-762)

An Lu-shan was the most powerful of these military governors, controlling all of northeast China. Although most people knew a rebellion was imminent, the self-involved emperor would hear nothing of it, so loyal forces were unprepared to defend the country. In December of 755, An Lu-shan's forces swept out of the northeast and quickly captured Lo-yang, the eastern capital, where An declared himself emperor of a new dynasty. The following summer, he captured Ch'ang-an.

Both cities were sacked brutally, and the devastation elsewhere was staggering.

Li Po fled to the south with his family and settled in the Hsün-yang area. In 757, Li Po became the presiding poet for a large force led by a certain Prince Lin, who had been sent to lead government resistance in the southeast. Eventually it became clear that the prince's true intention was to establish an independent regime in the south, and government armies engaged him in Yang-chou. His generals quickly abandoned him, as did Li Po, and the prince was soon defeated and executed.

Li Po made his way back to Hsün-yang, but he was there arrested as a traitor and jailed under sentence of death. Although the imprisonment lasted several months, he was finally exonerated. Not long afterwards, however, a new administration in Hsün-yang took a different view of his involvement with Prince Lin. Li Po, who was seriously ill, suddenly found himself banished to Yeh-lang in the far southwest.

Li Po was allowed to make the journey into exile at his leisure, and he made the best of it. He traveled up the Yangtze slowly, stopping often to visit friends and relatives. The chronology of Li Po's exile is vague, but it seems to have lasted about a year and a half. He eventually made the dangerous passage upstream through Three Gorges to K'uei-chou, which the Chinese considered to be on the very outskirts of the civilized world. The nearly impenetrable Wu Mountain complex which surrounded the city was inhabited by aboriginal tribes speaking dialects unintelligible to Han Chinese. Had Li

Po left K'uei-chou for Yeh-lang and the malarial south-lands, he would have entered a true banishment. Already sick, he would have expected to die there. Fortunately, he was pardoned while staying at K'uei-chou, and he promptly sailed back down the Yangtze to resume his life of wandering, though it was hardly the spontaneous and joyful wandering of his earlier years. Indeed, for the last eight years of his life, beginning with the outbreak of the An Lu-shan rebellion, Li Po wandered more as a sick refugee and exile than a carefree romantic.

Rebel forces, which had been pushed back into the northeast and seemed all but defeated, dealt government forces several severe defeats and began regaining territory, including Lo-yang. Meanwhile, with the central government foundering, opportunists throughout China began launching local revolts in the attempt to set up independent regimes in their regions, and Li Po had to flee several such revolts in his last years. Throughout this period of fighting, Li Po hoped and petitioned for an administrative position which would allow him to help the government defend itself against the rebels. And yet, in marked contrast to Tu Fu's work, Li Po's poetry reveals little concern with the fighting or the tremendous suffering it caused. The fall in census figures from 53 million before the fighting to only 17 million afterwards summarizes the rebellion's catastrophic impact. Of 53 million people, 36 million were left either dead or displaced and homeless. And although the rebellion itself ended in 763, the T'ang Dynasty never fully recovered from it and the chronic militarism it spawned.

In 762, a sick Li Po went to visit his "cousin" Li Yang-ping, one of the great T'ang calligraphers. It was the last in a lifetime of journeys. In the end, *tzu-jan* is the form of loss. Li Po arrived at Li Yang-ping's home with a confusion of rough drafts which, being desperately ill, he asked Li Yang-ping to edit and preserve. He had managed to keep only a few hundred of the several thousand poems he'd written, and these were in turn soon lost. Another collection, of unknown origin, was discovered and edited by Li Po's friend, Wei Hao, but it too was lost. Little is known about the history of these texts, or what transformations they underwent, until they were combined in a printed edition hundreds of years later. Meanwhile, poems and manuscripts scattered around the country were collected and edited, and many of them were presumably included in the combined edition, though no one knows how many were actually written by Li Po. Of the several thousand poems he is said to have written, the collection we now have contains only about 1100, and only a portion of these is authentic. So the large majority of Li Po's work was apparently lost, especially that written during the difficult years of the rebellion. (Had this work survived, Li Po might look a little more politically engaged than he now does.) Combined with the dubious authenticity of so many surviving poems and the lack of biographical information, this loss makes Li Po as much unknown as known, as much legend as history.

It may be just as well, for the legend Li Po made of himself is more consistent and compelling if he remains, like the moon, an enduring mystery. Whatever actually happened at Li Yang-ping's house in the winter of 762, Li Po died as the legend says he died: out drunk in a boat, he fell into a river and drowned trying to embrace the moon.

—D.H.

EARLY YEARS
(A.D. 701-742)

GOING TO VISIT TAI-T'IEN MOUNTAIN'S MASTER OF THE WAY WITHOUT FINDING HIM

A dog barks among the sounds of water.
Dew stains peach blossoms. In forests,

I sight a few deer, then at the creek,
hear nothing of midday temple bells.

Wild bamboo parts blue haze. A stream
hangs in flight beneath emerald peaks.

No one knows where you've gone. Still,
for rest, I've found two or three pines.

O-MEI MOUNTAIN MOON

O-mei Mountain moon half-full in autumn. Tonight,
its light filling the P'ing-ch'iang River current,

I leave Ch'ing-ch'i for Three Gorges. Thinking of you
without seeing you, I pass downstream of Yü-chou.

AT CHING-MEN FERRY, A FAREWELL

Crossing into distances beyond Ching-men,
I set out through ancient southlands. Here,

mountains fall away into wide-open plains,
and the river flows into boundless space.

The moon setting, heaven's mirror in flight,
clouds build, spreading to seascape towers.

Poor waters of home. I know how it feels:
ten thousand miles of farewell on this boat.

GAZING AT THE LU MOUNTAIN WATERFALL

1

Climbing west toward Incense-Burner Peak,
I look south and see a falls of water, a cascade

hanging there, three thousand feet high,
then seething dozens of miles down canyons.

Sudden as lightning breaking into flight,
its white rainbow of mystery appears. Afraid

at first the celestial Star River is falling,
splitting and dissolving into cloud heavens,

I look up into force churning in strength,
all power, the very workings of Creation.

It keeps ocean winds blowing ceaselessly,
shines a mountain moon back into empty space,

empty space it tumbles and sprays through,
rinsing green cliffs clean on both sides,

sending pearls in flight scattering into mist
and whitewater seething down towering rock.

Here, after wandering among these renowned
mountains, the heart grows rich with repose.

Why talk of cleansing elixirs of immortality?
Here, the world's dust rinsed from my face,

I'll stay close to what I've always loved,
content to leave that peopled world forever.

2

Sunlight on Incense-Burner kindles violet smoke.
Watching the distant falls hang there, river

headwaters plummeting three thousand feet in flight,
I see Star River falling through nine heavens.

VISITING A CH'AN MASTER AMONG MOUNTAINS AND LAKES

Like Hui-yüan fostering Ling-yün,
you open the gates of Ch'an for me:

here beneath rock and pine, serene,
it's no different than Glacier Peak.

Blossoms pure, no dye of illusion,
mind and water both pure idleness,

I sit once and plumb whole kalpas,
see through heaven and earth empty.

NIGHT THOUGHTS AT TUNG-LIN MONASTERY ON LU MOUNTAIN

Alone, searching for blue-lotus roofs,
I set out from city gates. Soon, frost

clear, Tung-lin temple bells call out,
Hu Creek's moon bright in pale water.

Heaven's fragrance everywhere pure
emptiness, heaven's music endless,

I sit silent. It's still, the entire Buddha-
realm in a hair's-breadth, mind depths

all bottomless clarity, in which vast
kalpas begin and end out of nowhere.

SUNFLIGHT CHANT

Sun rises over its eastern harbor
as if coming from some underworld,
and crossing heaven, returns again to western seas,
nowhere its six sun-dragons could ever find rest.
It's kept up this daily beginning and ending forever,
but we're not made of such ancestral *ch'i,*
> so how long can we wander with it here?

Flowers bloom in spring wind. They never refuse.
And trees never resent leaf-fall in autumn skies.
No one could whip the turning seasons along so fast:
the ten thousand things rise and fall of themselves.

Hsi Ho, O great
Sun Mother, Sun Guide— how could you drown
> in those wild sea-swells of abandon?

And Lu Yang, by what power
halted evening's setting sun?
It defies Tao, offends heaven—
all fake and never-ending sham.
I'll toss this Mighty Mudball earth into a bag
and break free into that boundless birthchamber of it all!

WRITTEN ON A WALL AT SUMMIT-TOP TEMPLE

Staying the night at Summit-Top Temple,
you can reach out and touch the stars.

I venture no more than a low whisper,
afraid I'll wake the people of heaven.

CH'ANG-KAN VILLAGE SONG

These bangs not yet reaching my eyes,
I played at our gate, picking flowers,

and you came on your horse of bamboo,
circling the well, tossing green plums.

We lived together here in Ch'ang-kan,
two little people without suspicions.

At fourteen, when I became your wife,
so timid and betrayed I never smiled,

I faced wall and shadow, eyes downcast.
A thousand pleas: I ignored them all.

At fifteen, my scowl began to soften.
I wanted us mingled as dust and ash,

and you always stood fast here for me,
no tower vigils awaiting your return.

At sixteen, you sailed far off to distant
Yen-yü Rock in Ch'ü-t'ang Gorge, fierce

June waters impossible, and howling
gibbons called out into the heavens.

At our gate, where you lingered long,
moss buried your tracks one by one,

deep green moss I can't sweep away.
And autumn's come early. Leaves fall.

It's September now. Butterflies appear
in the west garden. They fly in pairs,

and it hurts. I sit heart-stricken
at the bloom of youth in my old face.

Before you start back from out beyond
all those gorges, send a letter home.

I'm not saying I'd go far to meet you,
no further than Ch'ang-feng Sands.

FAREWELL TO A VISITOR RETURNING EAST

Autumn rains ending in this river town,
and wine gone, your lone sail soars away.

Setting out across billows and waves, your
family settles back for the journey home

past islands lavish with blossoms ablaze,
willow filigree crowding in over the banks.

And after you're gone, nothing left to do,
I go back and sweep off the fishing pier.

ON YELLOW-CRANE TOWER, FAREWELL TO MENG HAO-JAN WHO'S LEAVING FOR YANG-CHOU

From Yellow-Crane Tower, my old friend leaves the west.
Downstream to Yang-chou, late spring a haze of blossoms,

distant glints of lone sail vanish into emerald-green air:
nothing left but a river flowing on the borders of heaven.

TO SEND FAR AWAY

So much beauty home— flowers filled the house.
So much beauty gone— nothing but this empty bed,

your embroidered quilt rolled up, never used.
It's been three years. Your scent still lingers,

your scent gone and yet never ending.
But now you're gone, never to return,

thoughts of you yellow leaves falling,
white dew glistening on green moss.

HSIANG-YANG SONGS

1

In Hsiang-yang, pleasures abound. They play
Copper-Blond Horses, and we sing and dance.

But it's a river town. Return to clear water,
and a blossoming moon bares our delusions.

2

Hsien Mountain rises above emerald Han River
waters and snow-white sand. On top, inscribed

to life's empty vanishing, a monument stands,
long since blotted out beneath green moss.

SOMETHING SAID, WAKING DRUNK
ON A SPRING DAY

It's like boundless dream here in this
world, nothing anywhere to trouble us.

I have, therefore, been drunk all day,
a shambles of sleep on the front porch.

Coming to, I look into the courtyard.
There's a bird among blossoms calling,

and when I ask what season this is,
an oriole's voice drifts on spring winds.

Overcome, verging on sorrow and lament,
I pour another drink. Soon, awaiting

this bright moon, I'm chanting a song.
And now it's over, I've forgotten why.

AT YÜAN TAN-CH'IU'S MOUNTAIN HOME

By nature, my old friend on East Mountain
treasures the beauty of hills and valleys.

Spring now green, you lie in empty woods,
still sound asleep under a midday sun,

your robes growing lucid in pine winds,
rocky streams rinsing ear and heart clean.

No noise, no confusion— all I want is
this life pillowed high in emerald mist.

1

A woman alone here east of Ch'ung-ling
while you stay among Han River islands,

I look out across bright blossoms all day:
a lit path of white stretching between us.

We made clouds-and-rain love our farewell,
then nothing but autumn grasses remained,

autumn grasses and autumn moths rising,
and thoughts of you all twilight sorrow.

Will I ever see you again, ever darken
this lamp as you loosen my gauze robes?

2

Short and tall, spring grasses lavish
our gate with green, as if passion-driven,

everything returned from death to life.
My burr-weed heart— it alone is bitter.

You'll know that in these things I see
you here again, planting our gardens

behind the house, and us lazily gathering
what we've grown. It's no small thing.

AT FANG-CH'ENG MONASTERY, DISCUSSING CH'AN WITH YÜAN TAN-CH'IU

Alone, in the vast midst of boundless
dream, we begin to sense something:

wind and fire stir, come whorling
life into earth and water, giving us

this shape. Erasing dark confusion,
we penetrate to the essential points,

reach Nirvana-illumination, seeing
this body clearly, without any fears,

and waking beyond past and future,
we soon know the Buddha-mystery.

What luck to find a Ch'an recluse
offering emerald wine. We seem lost

together here— no different than
mountains and clouds. A clear wind

opens pure emptiness, bright moon
gazing on laughter and easy talk,

blue-lotus roofs. Timeless longing
breaks free in a wandering glance.

WRITTEN WHILE WANDERING THE WHITE RIVER IN NAN-YANG, AFTER CLIMBING ONTO THE ROCKS

Morning up near White River origins,
and suddenly that human world's gone:

islands all ends-of-the-earth beauty,
river and sky a vast vacant clarity.

Ocean clouds leave the eye's farewell,
and the mind idle, river fish wander.

Chanting, I linger out a setting sun,
then return moonlit to a farmland hut.

I hoard the sky a setting sun leaves
and love this cold stream's clarity:

western light follows water away,
rippled current a wanderer's heart.

I sing, watch cloud and moon, empty
song soon long wind through pine.

SONG OF THE MERCHANT

On heaven's wind, a sea traveler
wanders by boat through distances.

It's like a bird among the clouds:
once gone, gone without a trace.

FRONTIER-MOUNTAIN MOON

Over Heaven Mountain, the bright moon
rises through a boundless sea of cloud.

A hundred thousand miles long, steady
wind scouring Jasper-Gate Pass howls.

Our armies moving down White-Ascent Road,
Mongols probing along Sky-Blue Seas—

soldiers never return from those forced
marches ending on battlefields. Countless

guards look out across moonlit borderlands,
thinking of home, their faces all grief.

And somewhere, high in a tower tonight,
a restless woman cries out in half-sleep.

A SUMMER DAY IN THE MOUNTAINS

Flourishing a white-feather fan
lazily, I go naked in green forests.

Soon, I've hung my cap on a cliff,
set my hair loose among pine winds.

LISTENING TO LU TZU-HSÜN PLAY THE *CH'IN* ON A MOONLIT NIGHT

The night's lazy, the moon bright. Sitting
here, a recluse plays his pale white *ch'in,*

and suddenly, as if cold pines were singing,
it's all those harmonies of grieving wind.

Intricate fingers flurries of white snow,
empty thoughts emerald-water clarities:

No one understands now. Those who could
hear a song this deeply vanished long ago.

SPRING THOUGHTS

When grasses in Yen ripple like emerald silk
and lush mulberry branches sag in Ch'in,

he'll still dream of coming home one day,
and I'll still be waiting, broken-hearted.

We're strangers, spring wind and I. Why is it
here, slipping inside my gauze bed-curtains?

ANCIENT SONG

Chuang-tzu dreams he's a butterfly,
and a butterfly becomes Chuang-tzu.

All transformation this one body,
boundless occurrence goes on and on:

it's no surprise eastern seas become
western streams shallow and clear,

or the melon-grower at Ch'ing Gate
once reigned as Duke of Tung-ling.

Are hopes and dreams any different?
We bustle around, looking for what?

WAITING FOR WINE THAT DOESN'T COME

Jade winejars tied in blue silk . . . .
What's taking that wineseller so long?

Mountain flowers smiling, taunting me,
it's the perfect time to sip some wine,

ladle it out beneath my east window
at dusk, wandering orioles back again.

Spring breezes and their drunken guest:
today, we were meant for each other.

MOUNTAIN DIALOGUE

You ask why I've settled in these emerald mountains,
and so I smile, mind at ease of itself, and say nothing.

Peach blossoms drift streamwater away deep in mystery:
it's another heaven and earth, nowhere among people.

GAZING INTO ANTIQUITY AT SU TERRACE

Fresh willows among old gardens and overgrown terraces,
clear song of chestnuts in wind: spring's unbearable.

There's nothing left now— only this West River moon
that once lit those who peopled the imperial Wu palace.

GAZING INTO ANTIQUITY IN YÜEH

Kou Chien shattered Wu, then returned to his Yüeh kingdom.
Noble warriors home again boasting brocade robes, palace

women like blossoms filled springtime galleries here.
There's nothing left now— only quail breaking into flight.

AVOIDING FAREWELL IN A CHIN-LING WINESHOP

Breezes filling the inn with willow-blossom scents,
elegant girls serve wine, enticing us to try it.

Chin-ling friends come to see me off, I try to leave
but cannot, so we linger out another cup together.

I can't tell anymore. Which is long and which short,
the river flowing east or thoughts farewell brings on?

WANDERING T'AI MOUNTAIN

In May, the imperial road level stone
setting out, I ascend T'ai Mountain.

A six-dragon sun crossing ten thousand
ravines, valley streams meandering away,

I leave horse tracks winding through
emerald peaks all green moss by now,

water bathing cliffs in spray, cascades
headlong in flight. Among wailing pines,

I gaze north at wild headwalls, tilting
rock crumbling away east, and over

stone gates standing closed, lightning
storms rise from the bottom of earth.

Higher up, I see islands of immortals,
sea-visions all silver and gold towers,

and on Heaven's Gate, chant devotions.
A pure ten-thousand-mile wind arrives,

and four or five jade goddesses come
drifting down from the nine distances.

Smiling, they entice me empty-handed,
pour out cup-loads of dusk-tinted cloud.

I bow, then bow again, deeper, ashamed
I haven't an immortal's talent. And yet,

boundless, I can dwindle time and space
away, losing the world in such distances!

CH'ANG-AN
AND MIDDLE YEARS
(A.D. 742-755)

CH'ING P'ING LYRICS

Waking in the gallery
at dawn, and told it's snowing,

I raise the blinds and gaze into pure good fortune.
Courtyard steps a bright mirage of distance,

kitchen smoke trails light through flurried skies,
and the cold hangs jewels among whitened grasses.

Must be heaven's immortals in a drunken frenzy,
grabbing cloud and grinding it into white dust.

JADE-STAIRCASE GRIEVANCE

Night long on the jade staircase, white
dew appears, soaks through gauze stockings.

She lets down crystalline blinds, gazes out
through jewel lacework at the autumn moon.

DRINKING ALONE BENEATH THE MOON

1

Among the blossoms, a single jar of wine.
No one else here, I ladle it out myself.

Raising my cup, I toast the bright moon,
and facing my shadow makes friends three,

though moon has never understood wine,
and shadow only trails along behind me.

Kindred a moment with moon and shadow,
I've found a joy that must infuse spring:

I sing, and moon rocks back and forth;
I dance, and shadow tumbles into pieces.

Sober, we're together and happy. Drunk,
we scatter away into our own directions:

intimates forever, we'll wander carefree
and meet again in Star River distances.

2

Surely, if heaven didn't love wine,
there would be no Wine Star in heaven,

and if earth didn't love wine, surely
there would be no Wine Spring on earth.

Heaven and earth have always loved wine,
so how could loving wine shame heaven?

I hear clear wine called enlightenment,
and they say murky wine is like wisdom:

once you drink enlightenment and wisdom,
why go searching for gods and immortals?

Three cups and I've plumbed the great Way,
a jarful and I've merged with occurrence

appearing of itself. Wine's view is lived:
you can't preach doctrine to the sober.

3

It's April in Ch'ang-an, these thousand
blossoms making a brocade of daylight.

Who can bear spring's lonely sorrows, who
face it without wine? It's the only way.

Success or failure, life long or short:
our fate's given by Changemaker at birth.

But a single cup evens out life and death,
our ten thousand concerns unfathomed,

and once I'm drunk, all heaven and earth
vanish, leaving me suddenly alone in bed,

forgetting that person I am even exists.
Of all our joys, this must be the deepest.

THINKING OF EAST MOUNTAIN

It's forever since I faced East Mountain.
How many times have roses bloomed there,

or clouds returned, and thinned away,
a bright moon setting over whose home?

TO SEND FAR AWAY

Far away, I think of Wu Mountain light,
blossoms ablaze and a clear warm river.

Still here, something always keeping me
here, I face clouded southlands in tears.

Heartless as ever, spring wind buffeted
my dream, and your spirit startled away.

Unseen, you still fill sight. News is brief,
and stretching away, heaven never ends.

THOUGHTS OF YOU UNENDING

Thoughts of you unending
here in Ch'ang-an,

crickets where the well mirrors year-end golds cry out
autumn, and under a thin frost, mats look cold, ice-cold.

My lone lamp dark, thoughts thickening, I raise blinds
and gaze at the moon. It renders the deepest lament

empty. But you're lovely as a blossom born of cloud,

skies opening away all bottomless azure above, clear
water all billows and swelling waves below. Skies endless

for a spirit in sad flight, the road over hard passes
sheer distance, I'll never reach you, even in dreams,

my ruins of the heart,
thoughts of you unending.

WANDERING UP LO-FU CREEK ON A SPRING DAY

At the canyon's mouth, I'm singing. Soon
the path ends. People don't go any higher.

I scramble up cliffs into impossible valleys,
and follow the creek back toward its source.

Up where newborn clouds rise over open rock,
a guest come into wildflower confusions,

I'm still lingering on, my climb unfinished,
as the sun sinks away west of peaks galore.

ON HSIN-P'ING TOWER

On this tower as I leave our homeland,
late autumn wounds thoughts of return,

and heaven long, a setting sun far off,
this cold clear river keeps flowing away.

Chinese clouds rise from mountain forests;
Mongol geese on sandbars take flight.

A million miles azure pure— the eye
reaches beyond what ruins our lives.

WATCHING A WHITE FALCON SET LOOSE

High in September's frontier winds, white
brocade feathers, the Mongol falcon flies

alone, a flake of snow, a hundred miles
some fleeting speck of autumn in its eyes.

SHANG MOUNTAIN, FOUR-RECLUSE PASS

Hair white, four old sages cragged high
and timeless as South Mountain itself,

bitterly sure among cloud and pine:
they're hidden deep, unrecognizable

here. Azure sky a cloud-swept window,
cliffwalls all kingfisher blue across:

dragons and tigers at war in the world
still, of themselves, come to rest here.

Ch'in losing the Way's bright mirror,
Han ascending into purple heavens:

when the sun's lost in rainbow shadow,
North Star following it into obscurity,

the sage spreads wings toward flight,
helping sun and moon light our world.

However venerable, they're gone now:
open scrolls on chests, darkness become

the source of change, untold darkness
gone vast and deep. The sounds of flight

fill heaven's highway. I look up into
traces all boundless antiquity leaves.

SPRING GRIEVANCE

On a white horse bridled in gold, I go east of Liao-hai,
spread embroidered quilts, fall asleep in spring winds.

The moon sets, lighting my porch, probing dark lamps.
Blossoms drift through the door, smile on my empty bed.

TEASING TU FU

Here on the summit of Fan-k'o Mountain, it's Tu Fu
under a midday sun sporting his huge farmer's hat.

How is it you've gotten so thin since we parted?
Must be all those poems you've been suffering over.

AT SHA-CH'IU, SENT TO TU FU

Now that I've come here, I wonder why.
This Sha-ch'iu life's lazy and carefree,

but in ancient trees near the city wall,
sounds of autumn still swell at evening.

Wine here never gets me drunk. And if
local songs rekindle a feeling, it's empty.

My thoughts of you are like the Wen River,
sent broad and deep on its journey south.

AT SHA-CH'IU, FAREWELL TO WEI PA
WHO'S LEAVING FOR THE WESTERN CAPITAL

You arrived, a traveler from Ch'ang-an,
and now, returning there, you leave.

Headlong wind carries my thoughts away,
filling trees there in the western capital,

uneasy. There's no saying how this feels,
or if we'll ever meet again. I look far

without seeing you— look, and it's all
mist-gathered mountains opening away.

SPUR OF THE MOMENT

Facing wine, I missed night coming on
and falling blossoms filling my robes.

Drunk, I rise and wade the midstream moon,
birds soon gone, and people scarcer still.

WAR SOUTH OF THE GREAT WALL

War last year at the Sang-kan's headwaters,
war this year on the roads at Ts'ung River:

we've rinsed weapons clean in T'iao-chih sea-swells,
pastured horses in T'ien Mountain's snowbound grasses,

war in ten-thousand-mile campaigns
leaving our Three Armies old and broken,

but the Hsiung-nu have made slaughter their own
                                 version of plowing.
It never changes: nothing since ancient times but
                      bleached bones in fields of yellow sand.

A Ch'in emperor built the Great Wall to seal Mongols out,
and still, in the Han, we're setting beacon fires ablaze.

Beacon fires ablaze everlasting,
no end to forced marches and war,

it's fight to the death in outland war,
wounded horses wailing, crying out toward heaven,

hawks and crows tearing at people,
lifting off to scatter dangling entrails in dying trees.

Tangled grasses lie matted with death,
but generals keep at it. And for what?

Isn't it clear that weapons are the tools of misery?
The great sages never waited until the need
                                    for such things arose.

DRINKING IN THE MOUNTAINS WITH A RECLUSE

Drinking together among mountain blossoms, we
down a cup, another, and yet another. Soon drunk,

I fall asleep, and you wander off. Tomorrow morning,
if you think of it, grab your *ch'in* and come again.

SENT TO MY TWO CHILDREN IN SHA-CH'IU

Here in Wu, mulberry leaves lush green,
silkworms have already slept three times.

My family's stayed behind in Sha-ch'iu,
no one to plant Kuei Mountain fields,

no one to do spring work, and here I am
wandering rivers, more and more dazed.

A south wind carries my heart back, its
flight coming to rest outside the upstairs

drinking-room, where a lone peach stands,
branches in leaf sweeping azure mist.

I planted it there before leaving them,
and now three years have slipped away:

it's already reached the upstairs windows,
but my travels haven't brought me back.

Our darling P'ing-yang picks blossoms
and leans against it, picks blossoms

and looks for a father she can't see,
her tears flowing the way springs flow.

And how fast he's grown— little Po-ch'in
standing shoulder-high to his big sister!

My two kids under that peach together—
who comforts them with loving hugs now?

The sense of things blank, grief burning
through me day after day, I measure out

silk and write these far-away thoughts
sent traveling the Wen-yang River home.

IN THE STONE GATE MOUNTAINS, GONE LOOKING FOR YÜAN TAN-CH'IU

No plans to go looking for such solitude,
I set out on a whim, never mind distance.

Hiking up through boundless cliffs hard,
broad daylight's fading away in no time,

and before I pass three or four mountains,
the path's taken a million twists and turns.

In silence, deep silence, a gibbon shrieks.
I walk on and on, watching clouds build,

then a perfect moon clears towering pines,
opening autumn clarity into an empty valley.

There's still old snow in ravines up here,
and cold streams begin among broken rock.

Countless peaks deep in heaven, I climb on,
gazing into them, but they're inexhaustible.

Then Tan-ch'iu calls out in these distances,
and spotting me, breaks into a sudden smile.

Watchful, I cross into this valley, seeing
in it the ease you've mastered in stillness,

and soon we're lingering out ageless night,
leaving talk of return for clear dawn light.

IMPROMPTU CHANT

Dinner brings the savor of country fields,
and serving wine, we pour distant waters.

Watching the river flow east inexhaustibly
here, we can *see* how this farewell feels.

WAR SOUTH OF THE GREAT WALL

Delirium, battlefields all dark and delirium,
convulsions of men swarm like armies of ants.

A red wheel in thickened air, the sun hangs
above bramble and weed blood's dyed purple,

and crows, their beaks clutching warrior guts,
struggle at flight, grief-glutted, earthbound.

Those on guard atop the Great Wall yesterday
became ghosts in its shadow today. And still,

flags bright everywhere like scattered stars,
the slaughter keeps on. War-drums throbbing:

my husband, my sons— you'll find them all
there, out where war-drums keep throbbing.

FAREWELL TO YIN SHU

We drink deeply beneath dragon bamboo,
our lamp faint, the moon cold again.

On the sandbar, startled by drunken song,
a snowy egret lifts away past midnight.

CHING-T'ING MOUNTAIN, SITTING ALONE

The birds have all vanished into deep
skies. The last cloud drifts away, aimless.

Inexhaustible, Ching-t'ing Mountain and I
gaze at each other, it alone remaining.

AT HSÜAN-CHOU, I CLIMB HSIEH T'IAO'S NORTH TOWER IN AUTUMN

This river town could be in a painting:
mountains at dusk, clear-sky views empty.

Two rivers inscribing a lit inlay of mirror,
a pair of fallen rainbows for bridges,

kitchen-smoke veins cold orange groves,
and autumn stains ancient *wu-tung* trees.

Who'll remember someone facing wind
on North Tower, thinking of Hsieh T'iao?

AT HSIEH T'IAO'S HOUSE

A lingering, Ch'ing Mountain sun sinks.
It's all silence at Hsieh T'iao's home now:

sounds of people among bamboo gone,
the moon mirrored white in a pool empty.

Dry grasses fill the deserted courtyard.
Green moss shrouds the forgotten well.

Nothing stirs but the clarity of breezes
playing mid-stream across water and stone.

HEAVEN'S-GATE MOUNTAIN

Mountains set apart over the river,
two peaks face each other. Reflecting

chill colors of shoreline pine, waves
shatter apart into rock-torn bloom.

Heaven's distant borders ragged, haze
beyond clear sky and flushed cloud,

the sun sinks, a boat far off leaving
as I turn my head, deep in azure mist.

ON HSIEH T'IAO'S TOWER IN HSÜAN-CHOU: A FAREWELL DINNER FOR SHU YÜN

Leaving our departures behind, yesterday's
                  sunlight is light I couldn't hold back,
and throwing my heart into confusion, today's
                  sunlight is light bringing tangled sorrows.

Facing ten-thousand-mile winds, autumn geese leaving,
we can still laugh and drink in this tower tonight,

chant poems of Immortality Land, ancient word-bones.
The clarity of Hsieh T'iao reappears here among us:

all embracing, thoughts breaking free into flight,
we ascend azure heaven, gaze into a bright moon.

But slice water with a knife, and water still flows,
empty a winecup to end grief, and grief remains grief.

You never get what you want in this life, so why not
shake your hair loose on a boat at play in dawn light?

MOURNING OLD CHI, HSÜAN-CHOU'S MASTER WINEMAKER

Down there in graveland, old Chi
goes on making his Old Spring wine.

Dawn never cuts night short there,
but who comes to buy your wine now?

LISTENING TO A MONK'S *CH'IN* DEPTHS

Carrying a *ch'in* cased in green silk, a monk
descended from O-mei Mountain in the west.

When he plays, even in a few first notes,
I hear the pines of ten thousand valleys,

and streams rinse my wanderer's heart clean.
Echoes linger among temple frost-fall bells,

night coming unnoticed in emerald mountains,
autumn clouds banked up, gone dark and deep.

MOURNING CHAO

Chao left our imperial city for his Japanese homeland,
a lone flake of sail. Now he wanders islands of immortals.

Foundering in emerald seas, a bright moon never to return
leaves white, grief-tinged clouds crowding our southlands.

DRUNK ON T'UNG-KUAN MOUNTAIN, A QUATRAIN

I love this T'ung-kuan joy. A thousand
years, and still I'd never leave here.

It makes me dance, my swirling sleeves
sweeping all Five-Pine Mountain clean.

ON AUTUMN RIVER, ALONG PO-KO SHORES

1

Where could evening wandering be so fine?
Here along Po-ko shores, the moon bright,

mountain light trembles on drifted snow,
and gibbon shadow hangs from cold branches.

Only when this exquisite light dies away,
only then I turn my oars and start back.

When I came, it was such bright clear joy.
Now, it's all these thoughts of you again.

2

In the Po-ko night, a long wind howls.
Streams and valleys turn suddenly cold.

Fish and dragons roaming shoreline waters,
billows surge and waves swell everywhere.

Though heaven's loaned its moon, bright
moon come soaring over emerald clouds,

I can't see my old home anywhere. Heart-
stricken, I face west and look and look.

1

Long like autumn, all desolate silence,
Autumn River will return you to sorrow.

Unable to gauge this wanderer's sorrow,
I climb Ta-lou Mountain to the east

and gaze west into Ch'ang-an distances.
Looking down at the river flowing past,

I call out to its waters: *So how is it*
you'll remember nothing of me, and yet

you'd carry this one handful of tears
so very far— all the way to Yang-chou?

2

Autumn River's white gibbons seem countless,
a dancing flurry of leaps, snowflakes flying:

coaxing kids out of the branches, they descend,
and in a frolic, drink at the moon in water.

3

Wandering Autumn River in sorrow, I gaze into
Autumn River blossoms fiercely. Soon, it rivals

Yen-hsien for lovely mountains and streams,
and for wind and sun, it's another Ch'ang-sha.

4

Of these thousand-fold Autumn River peaks,
Waterwheel Mountain's unrivaled: heaven

tipped over, rock nearly pouring down,
and the water sweeps trees clean of moss.

5

There's a flake of rock on Chiang-tzu Peak,
a painted screen azure heaven sweeps clean.

The poem inscribed here keeps all boundless
antiquity alive— green words in moss brocade.

6

A million rock-cedars spread away here,
a hundred million stands of privet trees,

and white egrets fill endless mountains.
But white gibbons on stream after stream

howl. Stay away from Autumn River:
gibbon cries shatter a wanderer's heart.

7

Sentinel Rock mid-stream at Bird-Path Mountain,
Ancestor River appearing at Angler Bridge—

in wild water, the boat flies downstream,
mountain-flower scents rinsing my face clean.

8

The river's a bolt of bleached silk,
and earth stretches away into heaven.

I can ride bright moonlight, ascend
on this wine-boat, gazing at blossoms.

9

The pellucid moon in crystalline water
brightening, a snowy egret takes flight.

He heard her gathering chestnuts. Singing
in the night, they share the road home.

10

Smelter fires light up heaven and earth,
red stars swirling through purple smoke.

In the moonlit night, men's faces flushed,
worksong echoes out over the cold river.

11

Thirty thousand feet of white hair . . . .
It seems grief began that long ago,

and yet, in the bright mirror I wonder
where all this autumn frost came from.

12

Hardly ashore at Clear Creek, I hear it:
clarity, a voice of such perfect clarity.

At dusk, in farewell to a mountain monk,
I bow in deep reverence to white cloud.

ON AUTUMN RIVER AT CLEAR CREEK, FACING WINE IN THE SNOWY NIGHT: ONE OF US CAN CALL OUT IN PARTRIDGE SONG

Loosening my sable cloak, I face
white-jade winejars. Snowflakes

melt into our wine, and suddenly
it seems night cold isn't so cold.

A visitor here from Kuei-yang
calls mountain partridge. Clear

wind rustles bamboo at the window.
Peacock cries start breaking out.

This is music enough. Why tell
flutes and pipes our troubles?

CLEAR CREEK CHANT

It renders the mind clear— Clear Creek,
its water unrivaled for such pure color.

I can gaze into the bottom of its always
fresh repose. Is there anything like this

brilliant mirror in which people walk?
It's a wind-painting birds cross through,

and at nightfall, shrieking monkeys leave
all lament over distant wandering empty.

VISITING SHUI-HSI MONASTERY

Heaven Temple, Shui-hsi Monastery:
east wall lit beneath cloud brocade,

sounds of a clear stream tumbling past,
green bamboo harboring tower rooms.

The day unfettered under a cool wind,
we recluse guests mostly take it easy:

we think of sable-fur robes, chat about
autumn frost-fall, though it's only June,

old rock vines spreading, new leaves
opening on shoreline bamboo-shoots.

Chanting lazily, heart growing empty,
you think of all this and write lovely

lines. Everyone admires your poems,
rhymes floating boundless and clear.

Come here just this once, how is it I'm
content in Snow Mountain's answer?

WAR, EXILE,
AND LATER YEARS
(A.D. 755-762)

ON PHOENIX TOWER IN CHIN-LING

In its travels, the phoenix stopped at Phoenix Tower,
but soon left the tower empty, the river flowing away.

Blossoms and grasses burying the paths of a Wu palace,
Chin's capped and robed nobles all ancient gravemounds,

the peaks of Triple Mountain float beyond azure heavens,
and midstream in open waters, White-Egret Island hovers.

It's all drifting clouds and shrouded sun. Lost there,
our Ch'ang-an's nowhere in sight. And so begins grief.

AT CHIN-LING

Tucked into the earth, Chin-ling City,
the river curving past, flowing away:

there were once a million homes here,
and red towers along narrow lanes.

A vanished country all spring grasses
now, the palace buried in ancient hills,

this moon remains, facing the timeless
island across Hou Lake waters, empty.

ANCHORED OVERNIGHT AT NIU-CHU, THINKING OF ANCIENT TIMES

On West River at Niu-chu, night comes
all deep blue heavens, no trace of cloud.

From our boat, I watch the autumn moon,
hopes that Hsieh An's army will rescue

China empty. However immortal my song,
he'd never hear it, never come. At dawn,

we'll raise our sails into wind, sunlit
maple leaves falling and scattering away.

AFTER AN ANCIENT POEM

Years turn suddenly. Frost thickening
on Mongol winds, heaven and earth

converge. Grasslands facing a winter
moon dead, the six-dragon sun falls

beyond western wastes. Comets scatter
ethereal light. Venus rises in the east.

And somehow we've flown to safety here,
a pair of ducks in foreign southlands.

In the old days, it was falcons and dogs
for killing, now it's dukes and kings,

flood-dragons roaming all our waters,
fighting for ponds, seizing phoenixes—

and Northern Dipper never pours wine,
nor Southern Winnow fill with grain.

WRITTEN ON A WALL AT HSIU-CHING
MONASTERY IN WU-CH'ANG

Now a monastery on southern river-banks,
this was once my northern kinsman's home.

There's no one like him now. Courtyards
empty, monks sit deep in temple silence.

His books remain, bound in ribbon-grass,
and white dust blankets his *ch'in* stand.

He lived simply, planting peach and plum,
but in nirvana, springtime never arrives.

DRINKING WITH SHIH LANG-CHUNG, I HEAR A FLUTE ON YELLOW-CRANE TOWER SING

Leaving Wu-ch'ang alone, an exile sent wandering away,
I gaze west toward Ch'ang-an, home nowhere in sight.

On Yellow-Crane Tower, there's a jade-pure flute singing
in this river town, this fifth month, *Plum Blossoms Falling*.

9/9, OUT DRINKING ON DRAGON MOUNTAIN

9/9, out drinking on Dragon Mountain,
I'm an exile among yellow blossoms smiling.

Soon drunk, I watch my cap tumble in wind,
dance in love— a guest the moon invites.

Yesterday was our grand scale-the-heights day,
and this morning I'm tipping the cup again.

Poor chrysanthemum. No wonder you're so bitter,
suffering our revels these two days straight.

TRAVELING SOUTH TO YEH-LANG, SENT TO
MY WIFE IN YÜ-CHANG

This separation hurts, and Yeh-lang is beyond sky.
Moonlight fills the house, but news never comes.

I watched geese disappear north in spring, and now
they're coming south, but no letter from Yü-chang.

Azure heaven pinched between Wu Mountains,
riverwater keeps streaming down like this,

and with riverwater cascading so suddenly
away, we'll never reach that azure heaven.

Three mornings we start up Huang-niu Gorge,
and three nights find we've gone nowhere.

Three mornings and three nights: for once
I've forgotten my hair turning white as silk.

BEFORE MY BOAT ENTERS CH'Ü-T'ANG GORGE AND I LEAVE EASTERN PA BEHIND, I CLIMB THE HIGHEST WU MOUNTAIN PEAK. RETURNING LATE, I WRITE THIS ON A WALL

After traveling thousands of river miles,
a sea-born moon rising full fifteen times,

I'm about to start up Ch'ü-t'ang Gorge,
so I stop to hike among Wu Mountain peaks,

Wu Mountain peaks towering inexhaustibly
above Pa lands stretching away, limitless.

I climb fringes of sunlight, clutching vines,
and rest on rocky heights up beyond mist,

then race on, soon reaching the cragged
summit. There, no haze to the end of sight,

I look down cinnabar valleys left behind,
then up into azure heaven I've come so near,

azure heaven— if I could reach it, I could
sail away who knows where on the Star River.

Gazing at clouds, I know Shun's ancient tomb,
and river thoughts reach earth-cradling seas.

Wandering around, so much to see in late
lonesome light, quiet thoughts grow countless.

Snowdrifts blaze, lighting empty valleys,
and the wind sings through forest trees.

On the trail home, twilight comes. And yet,
the beauty of things still doesn't rest.

Gibbons call early along the cold river,
the moon among pine shadows already risen

and boundless, how boundless— moonlight,
and the sorrow in a gibbon's pure cry,

unbearable as I toss my walking-stick aside
and leave the mountains for this lone boat.

MAKING MY WAY TOWARD YEH-LANG IN EXILE, I REMEMBER WALKING AMONG PEACH BLOSSOMS LONG AGO AT AUTUMN RIVER

Peaches in blossom, spring waters high,
white stones appear, then sink away,

and rustling wisteria branches sway,
a half moon drifting azure heaven.

Who knows how many fiddleheads wait,
clenched along paths I once walked?

In three years, back from Yeh-lang,
I'll resolve my bones into gold there.

LEAVING K'UEI-CHOU CITY EARLY

Leaving K'uei-chou behind among dawn-tinted clouds,
I return a thousand miles to Chiang-ling in a day:

suddenly, no end to gibbons on both banks howling,
my boat's breezed past ten thousand crowded peaks.

TRAVELING TUNG-T'ING LAKE WITH CHIA CHIH AND MY UNCLE, LI YEH

1

Not a trace of mist on this southern lake tonight,
we could sail for heaven across autumn waters.

Let's follow distant Tung-t'ing moonlight all the way
and bargain for wine off among the white clouds.

2

Shun's wives came to bury him and never returned.
Gone among Tung-t'ing's autumn grasses, they're goddesses

now. A jade mirror sweeps open across the bright lake,
and in a pure-color painting, Goddess Mountain appears.

AFTER CLIMBING PA-LING MOUNTAIN, IN
THE WEST HALL AT K'AI-YÜAN MONASTERY:
OFFERED TO A MONK BEYOND THIS WORLD
ON HENG MOUNTAIN

There's a sage monk on Heng Mountain,
the beauty of five peaks his true bones,

autumn moon alight in a sea of water
revealing his ten-thousand-mile heart.

A guardian gone into southern darkness,
pilgrims of the Way all visit him there,

sweet dew sprinkling down, a language
clear and cool gracing flesh and hair.

Bright lake a mirror of fallen heaven,
scented hall a gate into all this silver:

come for the view, I feed on kind winds,
new blossoms teaching mind this vast.

AT LUNG-HSING MONASTERY, CHIA AND I CUT BRANCHES FROM AN *WU-T'UNG* TREE, THEN GAZE AT YUNG LAKE

The green *wu-t'ung*'s branches down,
we can sit looking out at Yung Lake.

Autumn mountains bathed pure in rain,
forests radiant, soaked in emerald quiet,

its bright mirror of water turns lazily
in a painted screen of changing cloud.

A thousand eras lost to wind, and still
the great sages all share this moment.

WRITTEN ON THE WALL WHILE DRUNK AT WANG'S HOUSE NORTH OF THE HAN RIVER

I'm like some partridge or quail—
going south, then flying lazily north.

And now I've come to find you here,
a little wine returns me to the moon.

LOOKING FOR YUNG, THE RECLUSE MASTER

Emerald peaks polish heaven. I wander,
sweeping clouds away, forgetting years,

looking for the ancient Way. Resting
against a tree, I listen to streamwater,

black ox dozing among warm blossoms,
white crane asleep in towering pines.

A voice calls through river-tinted dusk,
but I've descended into cool mist alone.

AFTER AN ANCIENT POEM

We the living, we're passing travelers:
it's in death alone that we return home.

All heaven and earth a single wayhouse,
the changeless grief of millennia dust,

moon-rabbit's immortality balm is empty,
and the timeless *fu-sang* tree kindling.

Bleached bones lie silent, say nothing,
and how can ever-green pines see spring?

Before and after pure lament, this life's
phantom treasure shines beyond knowing.

GAZING AT CRAB-APPLE MOUNTAIN

Up early, I watched the sun rise again.
At dusk, I watched birds return to roost.

A wanderer's heart sours bitterly. And here
on Crab-Apple Mountain, it's only worse.

FACING WINE

Never refuse wine. I'm telling you,
people come smiling in spring winds:

peach and plum like old friends, their
open blossoms scattering toward me,

singing orioles in jade-green trees,
and moonlight probing gold winejars.

Yesterday we were flush with youth,
and today, white hair's an onslaught.

Bramble's overgrown Shih-hu Temple,
and deer roam Ku-su Terrace ruins:

it's always been like this, yellow dust
choking even imperial gates closed

in the end. If you don't drink wine,
where are those ancient people now?

DRINKING ALONE ON A SPRING DAY

1

East wind fans clear, warm air through
shoreline trees ablaze with spring color,

and sunlight shimmers in green grasses,
falling blossoms scattering into flight.

Lone cloud returning to empty mountains,
birds returning, each to its own home:

in all this, nothing is without refuge.
I alone have nowhere in life to turn.

Forever drunk, I face rock-born moon,
sing for wildflower sights and smells.

2

Flushed clouds of wandering immortals
fill my thoughts, and all their island

distances. Facing a winejar, boundless
occurrence settling into lazy repose,

I lay my *ch'in* against a towering pine
and gaze to far mountains, cup in hand.

Birds leaving vanish into endless sky.
The sun sets. A lone cloud returns.

It's just that, here in this failing light,
long ago flares into colors of autumn.

A FRIEND STAYS THE NIGHT

Rinsing sorrows of a thousand forevers
away, we linger out a hundred jars of wine,

the clear night's clarity filling small talk,
a lucid moon keeping us awake. And after

we're drunk, we sleep in empty mountains,
all heaven our blanket, earth our pillow.

SPENDING THE NIGHT BELOW WU-SUNG MOUNTAIN, IN OLD MRS. HSÜN'S HOUSE

Overnight below Wu-sung, I find empty
quiet's brought no one joy, and autumn

harvest only means farmhouses in grief,
neighbor women out pounding grain cold.

She bows before serving us watergrass,
radiant moonlight filling empty plates.

A mother cast so adrift shames the world:
out pleading three times and still no food.

FAREWELL TO HAN SHIH-YÜ WHO'S LEAVING
FOR HUANG-TE

Where's the splendor in embroidered robes of long ago?
Wine's bought on credit tonight, but we're together,

and in an instant, East Mountain's all borrowed moonlight.
All night drunk, we sing farewell to a moonlit stream.

DRINKING ALONE

As if they could feel, spring grasses
turn shade beside the house jade-green.

When this east wind blows, grief comes.
I sit out in its bluster, my hair white,

and drink alone, inviting my shadow.
Chanting lazily, I face trees in flower.

Old pine, what have you learned? Cold,
cold and desolate— who's your song for?

On stone, fingers in moonlight dance
over the *ch'in* in my lapful of blossoms.

Out beyond this jar of wine, it's all
longing, longing— no heart of mine.

SEEING THAT WHITE-HAIRED OLD MAN LEGEND
DESCRIBES IN COUNTRY GRASSES

After wine, I go out into the fields,
wander open country— singing,

asking myself how green grass
could be a white-haired old man.

But looking into a bright mirror,
I see him in my failing hair too.

Blossom scent seems to scold me.
I let grief go, and face east winds.

THOUGHTS IN NIGHT QUIET

Seeing moonlight here at my bed,
and thinking it's frost on the ground,

I look up, gaze at the mountain moon,
then back, dreaming of my old home.

LINES THREE, FIVE, SEVEN WORDS LONG

Autumn wind clear,
autumn moon bright,

fallen leaves gather in piles, then scatter,
and crows settling-in, cold, startle away.

Will we ever see, ever even think of each other again?
This night, this moment: impossible to feel it all.

SOUTH OF THE YANGTZE, THINKING OF SPRING

How many times will I see spring green
again, or yellow birds tireless in song?

The road home ends at the edge of heaven.
Here beyond the river, my old hair white,

my heart flown north to cloudy passes,
I'm shadow in moonlit southern mountains.

My life a blaze of spent abundance, my old
fields and gardens buried in weeds, where

am I going? It's year's-end, and I'm here
chanting long farewells at heaven's gate.

ON GAZING INTO A MIRROR

Follow Tao, and nothing's old or new.
Lose it, and the ruins of age return.

Someone smiling back in the mirror,
hair white as the frost-stained grass,

you admit lament is empty, ask how
reflections get so worn and withered.

How speak of peach and plum: timeless
South Mountain's blaze in the end?

NOTES

6   STAR RIVER: the Milky Way.
CREATION: literally "create change" (*tsao-hua*), the force driving the ongoing process of change—a kind of deified principle.

8   HUI YÜAN: A major figure in the history of Chinese Buddhism, Hui Yüan (334-416) emphasized *dhyana* (sitting meditation), teaching a form of Buddhism which contained early glimmers of Ch'an (Zen).
LING-YÜN: Hsieh Ling-yün (385-433), the great pre-T'ang poet (see Introduction). When he first visited Hui Yüan in the Lu Mountains at his Tung-lin Monastery (see following poem), Ling-yün's "heart submitted to him reverently." Hsieh Ling-yün thereupon joined Hui Yüan's spiritual community, and Buddhism became central to his life and work.
KALPA: In Ch'an, the term for an endlessly long period of time. Originally, in Vedic scripture, a kalpa is a world-cycle lasting 4,320,000 years.

10   CH'I: universal breath or life-giving principle.
HSI-HO: Hsi Ho drove the sun-chariot, which was pulled by six dragons.
LU YANG: Lu Yang's army was in the midst of battle as evening approached. Fearing nightfall would rob him of victory, Lu Yang shook his spear at the setting sun, and it thereupon reversed its course.

12   Translated by Ezra Pound as "The River-Merchant's Wife," this poem is a modernist classic. Indeed, translat-

ed under his Japanese name (Rihaku) in Pound's *Cathay*, Li Po was an important part of the modernist revolution Pound engineered. Nevertheless, there is no reason to think the husband is a river-merchant. The wandering Li Po was likely thinking figuratively of his own wife.

This poem is in the *yüeh-fu* form. Originally, *yüeh-fu* were folk songs, often critical of the government, which were collected by the Han emperor Wu's Music Bureau ("*yüeh-fu*" means "Music Bureau") to gauge the sentiments of the common people. Hence, as poets later adopted the form, using a common person as the poem's speaker became a convention. As here, the speaker is often a woman left alone by her lover (cf. 20-21, 29, 65). See also p. 58 and note.

15 MENG HAO-JAN: the eldest of the great High T'ang poets.

20 CLOUDS-AND-RAIN LOVE: From the legend of a prince who, while visiting Wu Mountain, was visited in his sleep by a beautiful woman who said that she was the goddess of Wu Mountain. She spent the night with him, and as she left said: "At dawn I marshal the morning clouds; at nightfall I summon the rain."

28 CH'IN: ancient stringed instrument which Chinese poets used to accompany the chanting of their poems. It is ancestor to the more familiar Japanese *koto*.

30 CHUANG-TZU ... BUTTERFLY: This story, in which Chuang-tzu can't decide whether he's Chuang-tzu dreaming he's a butterfly or a butterfly dreaming he's Chuang-tzu, is found at the end of Chapter 2 in the *Chuang Tzu*.
EASTERN SEAS ... WESTERN STREAMS: After China's rivers flow into the eastern sea, they ascend to become the Star River (Milky Way) and flow back across the sky to descend

again in the west, forming the headwaters of the rivers again.

33 Wu was an ancient kingdom in southeast China. The Wu emperor referred to in this poem is Fu Ch'a, whose weakness for beautiful women had disastrous consequences (much like Hsüan-tsung's infatuation with Yang Kuei-fei, which gives these poems a layer of topical political comment). The legendary beauty Hsi Shih was sent to Fu Ch'a by Kou Chien, ruler of Yüeh, Wu's rival kingdom to the south. Once Fu Ch'a had succumbed to her pleasures and neglected his kingdom, Yüeh invaded and conquered Wu (472 B.C.), a subject taken up in the following poem.

36 T'AI MOUNTAIN: There are five especially sacred mountains in China, one for each of the four directions and one at the center. T'ai, in the east, is perhaps the most revered of these mountains, and its summit the destination of many pilgrims. The T'ai Mountain complex includes many lower ridges and summits, one of which is Heaven's Gate.

41 Li Po's way of life often led him to inns and winehouses where courtesans entertained guests with a popular song-form called *tz'u*. Probably imported from Li Po's native central Asia, *tz'u* had been considered unfit for serious poets. Not surprisingly, Li Po was the first major poet to ignore this convention. Each *tz'u* had a different song-form, and poets would write lyrics that fit the music, which meant using quite irregular line lengths. Here, the title of the original *tz'u* is "*Ch'ing P'ing*," hence: "*Ch'ing P'ing Lyrics.*" *Tz'u* thereafter grew in importance as a serious poetic form, eventually becoming the distinctive form of the Sung Dynasty.

47 SPIRIT: It was thought that in sleep one's spirit could go off to visit someone else's dreams.

48 SPIRIT IN SAD FLIGHT: Although the spirit can go some distance during sleep or when a person suffers some emotional trauma, after death, it can travel long distances.

52 FOUR-RECLUSE PASS: Toward the end of the Ch'in Dynasty, four sages known as the "Four White-heads" retired to Shang Mountain near Lo-yang in protest of the tyrannical government. When the Han Dynasty replaced the Ch'in (206 B.C.), they still refused to leave the mountain.
SOUTH MOUNTAIN: Calling up such passages as "like the timelessness of South Mountain" in the *Book of Songs* (*Shih Ching*, 166/6), South Mountain came to have a kind of mythic stature as the embodiment of the elemental and timeless nature of the earth.

58 Another kind of *yüeh-fu*, the traditional form for poems of social protest, which allows rather extreme metrical irregularities. As is often the case with T'ang Dynasty *yüeh-fu*, it is set in the Han Dynasty—a convention used when the poem was likely to offend those in power (here the protest would be against the expansionist militarism of the government). The speaker here is a soldier.
HSIUNG-NU: war-like nomadic peoples occupying vast regions from Mongolia to Central Asia during the Han Dynasty. They were a constant menace on China's northern frontier.

60 CH'IN: see note for p. 28.

61 SILKWORMS ... SLEPT THREE TIMES: Silkworms, which feed on mulberry leaves, go through three or four cycles of feed-

ing and sleeping each spring and summer before spinning their cocoons.

68   HSIEH T'IAO: 5th-century poet remembered for his landscape poems.

74   CHAO: A native Japanese, Chao went to China as a young man to complete his education. He remained there and rose to high office. In A.D.753, he tried to return to Japan, but his ship was blown off course and wrecked. Chao survived, but when Li Po wrote this poem, it was apparently thought that he had perished.

91   PHOENIX: The mythic phoenix appears only in times of peace and sagacious rule, which was certainly not the case during the An Lu-shan rebellion when this poem was written.
     WU . . . CHIN: The ancient kingdom of Wu and the Chin Dynasty both had their capitals at Chin-ling.

93   HSIEH AN: One of Li Po's favorite historical figures, Hsieh An (A.D.320-385) lived as a scholar-recluse until the country's difficulties required that he enter government service. North China had already fallen to invading "barbarians." When their armies advanced on the south, Hsieh led an outnumbered Chinese army that repelled them, thereby saving China from being completely overrun.

94   NORTHERN DIPPER . . . SOUTHERN WINNOW: constellations.

95   KINSMAN: Li Yung, who was executed on trumped-up charges by Li Lin-fu, the notorious prime minister who was currently doing such damage to the country.

97   9/9: the 9th day of the 9th month, a holiday celebrated by

climbing to a mountaintop and drinking chrysanthemum wine, which was believed to enhance longevity.

99 GEESE: traditionally associated with letters from loved ones far away.

100 THREE GORGES: a set of three spectacular gorges formed where the Yangtze River cut its way through the formidable Wu Mountains, forming a two-hundred-mile stretch of very narrow canyons. Famous in Chinese poetry for the river's violence and the towering cliffs alive with shrieking gibbons, travel through them was very dangerous. The three gorges are: Ch'ü-t'ang Gorge, which begins at Kuei-chou; Wu Gorge; and furthest downsteam, Huang-niu Gorge, the first Li Po would encounter on his journey upstream.

101 SHUN: last emperor of China's legendary Golden Age (regnant 2255-2208 B.C.). After his death, the world began to decline.

109 BLACK OX . . . WHITE CRANE: animals the immortals typically rode in their celestial journeys.

110 MOON-RABBIT: According to popular myth, there is a rabbit on the moon under a cinnamon tree. There it pounds a balm of immortality using, among other things, sap and bark from the tree.

TIMELESS *FU-SANG* TREE: The sun is, also according to popular myth, ten crows— one for each day of the week. Each day, one sun-crow rises from the vast *fu-sang* (mulberry) tree in the far east. After setting, it waits in the tree's branches until its turn to rise comes again, ten days later.

123 SOUTH MOUNTAIN: see note for p. 52.

FINDING LIST

TEXTS:

1. *Li T'ai-po shih chi.* Wang Chi, ed. 1759. SPPY
   (*Chüan* and page number).
2. *Li Po chi chiao chu.* Ch'ü Shui-yüan, ed. 1980.
   (Page number; and for poems with multiple sections,
   section number in parenthesis).

PAGE	1. Li T'ai-po shih chi	2. Li Po chi chiao chu	PAGE	1. Li T'ai-po shih chi	2. Li Po chi chiao chu
3	23.10a	1355	28	23.7a	1345
4	8.12a	566	29	6.11a	448
5	15.18a	941	30	2.7b	110
6	21.11a	1238	31	23.5a	1340
8	20.12a	1180	32	19.2b	1095
9	23.8a	1349	33	22.11a	1291
10	3.28b	267	34	22.11b	1292
11	30.11a	1715	35	15.12b	928
12	4.19a	326	36	20.3a	1154(1)
14	30.7b	1708	41	30.5b	1727(3)
15	15.15b	935	42	5.12a	374
16	25.11a	1465(11)	43	23.2b	1331(1-3)
17	5.12a	374(1,3)	46	23.12b	1361
18	23.8a	1348	47	25.11a	1465(5)
19	25.1b	1438	48	3.19b	244
20	25.11a	1465(7,9)	49	20.9a	1170
22	23.1a	1325	50	21.5a	1222
23	20.1a	1149	51	24.21a	1422(1)
24	20.1a	1150	52	22.11b	1293
25	6.13a	455	53	25.14b	1476
26	4.1a	279	54	30.4b	1700
27	23.7b	1347	55	13.5b	836

BIBLIOGRAPHY

Alley, Rewi. *Li Pai: 200 Selected Poems*. Hong Kong: Joint Publishing, 1980.

Billeter, Jean François. *The Chinese Art of Writing*. New York: Rizzoli, 1990.

Pages 192-195 of this book contain a color reproduction of the only surviving piece of calligraphy that can be attributed to Li Po, as well as a splendid stroke-by-stroke description of how Li Po's character is revealed in his calligraphic art.

Birch, Cyril. *Anthology of Chinese Literature: From Early Times to the Fourteenth Century*. New York: Grove Press, 1965.

Cheng, François. *Chinese Poetic Writing: With an Anthology of T'ang Poetry*. Chinese trans. J. P. Seaton. Bloomington: Indiana Univ. Press, 1982.

Cooper, Arthur. *Li Po and Tu Fu*. Harmondsworth: Penguin Books, 1973.

Eide, Elling. "On Li Po." In *Perspectives on the T'ang*. New Haven: Yale Univ. Press, 1973.

——————. *Poems by Li Po*. Lexington: Anvil Press, 1984.

Hamill, Sam. *Banished Immortal: Visions of Li T'ai-po*. Fredonia: White Pine Press, 1987.

Liu Wu-chi, and Irving Yucheng Lo. *Sunflower Splendor: Three Thousand Years of Chinese Poetry*. Bloomington: Indiana Univ. Press, 1975.

Nienhauser, William. *The Indiana Companion to Traditional Chinese Literature*. Bloomington: Indiana Univ. Press, 1986.

Owen, Stephen. *The Great Age of Chinese Poetry: The High T'ang.* New Haven: Yale Univ. Press, 1981.

——————. *Traditional Chinese Poetry and Poetics.* Madison: Univ. of Wisconsin Press, 1985.

Pound, Ezra. "Cathay." In *Personæ: The Shorter Poems.* Revised edition. New York: New Directions, 1990.

Seaton, J. P. and James Cryer. *Bright Moon, Perching Bird: Poems by Li Po and Tu Fu.* Middletown: Wesleyan Univ. Press, 1987.

Shigenyoshi, Obata. *The Works of Li Po the Chinese Poet.* New York: Dutton, 1922.

T'ao Ch'ien. *The Selected Poems of T'ao Ch'ien.* Trans. David Hinton. Port Townsend: Copper Canyon Press, 1993.

Tu Fu. *The Selected Poems of Tu Fu.* Trans. David Hinton. New York: New Directions, 1989.

Waley, Arthur. *The Poetry and Career of Li Po 701-762 A.D.* London: Allen & Unwin, 1950.

Watson, Burton. *Chinese Lyricism.* New York: Columbia Univ. Press, 1971.

——————. *The Columbia Book of Chinese Poetry.* New York: Columbia Univ. Press, 1984.